DATE DUE

	DISCARD		

Everything
You Need to
Know About

Being a
Teen
Driver

You have probably been dreaming about the day you can finally drive for a long time!

Everything You Need to Know About Being a Teen Driver

Adam Winters

The Rosen Publishing Group, Inc.
New York

To Monty—who sat (silently) beside me as I zoomed around Mt. Pleasant cemetery—for long-lasting patience and support, both on the road and off.

Published in 2000 by The Rosen Publishing Group, Inc.
29 East 21st Street, New York, NY 10010

First Edition

Library of Congress Cataloging-in-Publication Data

Winters, Adam, 1951–
    Everything you need to know about being a teen driver / by Adam Winters. — 1st. ed.
        p. cm. (The need to know library)
Includes bibliographical references and index.
Summary: Discusses becoming a licensed driver and such related concerns as getting your first car, road safety, drinking and driving, and road rage.
    ISBN 0-8239-3287-7
    1. Automobile driving—Juvenile literature. 2. Teenage automobile drivers—Juvenile literature. [1. Automobile driving.] I. Title. II. Series.
    TL152.5 .W55 2000
    629.28'3—dc21

                                                          00-009102

Manufactured in the United States of America

Contents

Introduction

Ever since you were a little kid, with your toy cars and your red wagon, a four-wheeled automobile has probably been a part of your life. By the time you hit five or six, your mom or dad was perhaps letting you climb into the family car, spin the steering wheel, and make convincing *vrroom vrroom!* noises. Such experiences probably made you dream about the day when you would find yourself behind the wheel of your own wheels, zooming down a highway with the wind in your hair, music on the radio, free to drive all the way to the tip of South America if you wanted to.

It seemed as if you would never get to the age where you would be old enough to drive. But before you knew it, you were blowing out the candles on your sixteenth birthday cake and all your friends were asking you: "So when are you going to get your license?"

If you don't live in a big city with a good public transportation system, driving a car is an especially big deal. It means not being carted around by your parents, older siblings, or friends. It means freedom to go where you want, when you want. Even if you live in a big city where you need a car only once in a while, learning to drive—particularly in the United States—is like a rite of passage to becoming an adult. It means that (in theory) you are enough of a grown-up to drive around the streets and highways of this country with other adults.

Because driving is a "grown-up" activity, you should realize that—like most adult activities—there are plenty of responsibilities that go along with it. These range from making sure your car is in top shape to knowing the rules of the road and how to act and react to the millions of other drivers with whom you will come into contact. Some of these other drivers will be courteous, responsible, good drivers such as yourself. A few others will be rude, reckless, and they may sometimes break the rules.

Many of these bad drivers are adults. But unfortunately, a very large percentage are teenagers. Because of the frequency with which they speed, drink and drive, and take stupid risks, a significant number of car crashes involve teen drivers. This isn't only a question

Driving comes with many responsibilities, so be sure you are ready to keep your car in shape and abide by the rules of the road.

of adults getting on teens' cases—it has been statistically proven. The sad truth is that for every mile driven, a sixteen-year-old has twenty times as many crashes as the average adult. The resulting drawbacks for teens are that laws get tougher, insurance rates get higher, and young drivers as a whole get a bad reputation. So when you do finally find yourself behind the wheel of a car, try to prove both the stats and the rep wrong. Along with exploring many issues dealing with driving and cars in general, this book will give you some of the dos and don'ts that will help you to become a good, safe, confident driver.

Chapter One

So You Want to Drive?

Nobody is born knowing instinctively how to drive. If you want to master the ins and outs of passing, parking, and other motorized maneuvers, you have to learn—and learn well.

This is why in most states, before you can get a driver's license, you must get a learner's permit. A learner's permit is a temporary license that allows you to legally zoom around in a car, as long as you are accompanied by another licensed driver. In order to get a learner's permit, you have to pass an eye exam and a multiple choice test with questions pertaining to rules of the road in your state. To study for this test, you'll need to pick up a Driver's Manual from your state's Department of Motor Vehicles (DMV).

Driver's Ed

Once you have your permit, there's no stopping you. With that little slip of paper, you (and the brave soul you recruit to sit by your side) will be able to take to the asphalt in no time. At the same time, while you are learning the ropes you should also enroll in a driving class.

"Driver's ed" is driver's education, the courses that aspiring drivers need to take in order to learn how to drive. In most states, this education is essential—you can't get your license without first having taken the necessary amount of required classes. Generally, these include learning about rules of the road and safety in the classroom, and learning practical techniques such as parallel parking and three-point turns on an actual road.

It used to be that most driver's ed courses were publicly funded by your state. This meant that for a small fee, you could take courses with your pals at school. Unfortunately, many states have cut funding for driver's education. In the meantime, lots of private driving schools have opened up. Although more expensive—some people complain that now only those who can afford to will learn how to drive safely—these schools often have more flexible timetables, as well as better facilities. Sometimes, completing a course will give you a reduction in your insurance policy.

Driver's education includes learning about safety and road rules, as well as practical techniques such as parallel parking.

Practice Makes Perfect

Completing driver's ed doesn't mean you're suddenly Tom Cruise in *Days of Thunder*. Most experts agree that many teen car crashes are not the result of drinking and driving or speeding, but of sheer inexperience.

It takes practice and experience to be a good driver. Even armed with an expensive pro racket and the most high-tech sneakers imaginable, you can't expect to walk onto a tennis court and, within a few weeks, have the lightning reflexes of Martina Hingis or the powerful serve of Andre Agassi. Same deal with a car. Just because you've got a few lessons under your belt and are behind the wheel of a powerful car, it doesn't mean you're ready to rule the road.

Driver's education is an essential part of learning how to drive. But like any lessons you take—whether banjo or ballet—you have to try out the skills you learn on your own in order to perfect them. When it comes to driving, you probably know that it is against the law to zoom around solo before you have your license. But in most states, with a learner's permit, you can drive provided that your experienced mom, dad, older sister, uncle Louis, or grandmother is buckled in beside you. In fact, the more time—and patience—you can con these charitable elders into donating, the better driver you will be.

Because sixteen-year-old drivers crash more than those in any other age group, many motor safety groups think that driver's ed isn't doing a very good job of training safe drivers. Even the American Automobile Association's (AAA) Foundation for Traffic Safety has been critical of driver's ed. When a recent AAA study came up with some new ways of turning kids into better drivers, number one on the list was having a parent in the front seat. It seems that stricter laws, tougher driving exams, and longer driver's ed courses haven't had much impact. According to a report published by the University of North Carolina's Highway Safety Research Center, one out of every four sixteen-year-olds has some kind of crash in his or her first year of driving.

Of course some parents do find it stressful to sit, powerless, in the front seat while their "babies" are spinning the wheel of the family cruiser. The slightest jerk, lurch, or unsignaled turn can fill nervous parents with visions of crumpled hoods and bent fenders. That is why it's a good idea to select the adult who accompanies you with some thought to how calm and confident that person will make you feel (as well as how well they themselves drive). If a parent is going to stress you out and distract you, substitute another relative, a family friend, or even a pal's parent.

The Big Test

So you're at the stage where you can back out of the driveway wearing a blindfold and you can recite every rule of the road at the speed of seventy miles an hour. If you and your parents (and your driving teacher) think you're up to it—then it's time for the Big Test.

Depending on where you live, you will have to make an appointment well in advance to take your driving test. In some places and at certain times of the year, you can book a date a week beforehand. In other places and at other times, you might have to wait some months. What you can usually depend upon, however, is being pretty nervous when the actual date finally rolls around.

Sixteen-year-old Drew woke up with mega butterflies in his stomach on the day of his driving test. Scratch the butterflies—they were more like winged elephants. Thinking Drew would feel more confident taking the test in a car with which he was familiar instead of one supplied by the Department of Motor Vehicles, his dad had promised to lend him the family car. Nevertheless, Drew was sure he was going to forget something basic.

Drew had to force himself to eat the "Good Luck!" breakfast his mom had made for him. He could barely swallow at all. "Relax, son," said his mom, planting a plate of blueberry pancakes in front of Drew. "Just think that with all the practice you've had, you're already a much better driver than the majority of lunatics out there on the road." But Drew wasn't reassured. If he didn't get his license today, he would be the laughing stock of the whole school.

Just as he was about to leave the house, the phone rang. It was his best friend Leona, calling to wish him good luck. "I'm nervous that I'll have this real tough examiner," he confessed to Leona. "Just imagine the guy is sitting beside you in his boxers," advised Leona. "That's what I did, and it really worked."

An hour later, when a short, bald, and pudgy man named Mr. Wade climbed into his car, Drew felt nervous. "Well, what are you waiting for, kid?" asked the examiner, looking at his watch. "Get on with it." Drew plunged the car keys into the ignition, turned, and then, pressing down too hard on the gas pedal, he suddenly plunged forward. Mr. Wade shot him a dirty look and Drew was sure he was doomed to fail. Then he thought of Leona's advice. As he carefully put the car into reverse, he stopped to look at Mr. Wade and was thrilled to discover that the man was sitting there in the ugliest pair of light green underwear he had ever set eyes upon.

Weirdly enough, after this vision, Drew suddenly felt the panic drain out of him. In fact, he almost felt like chuckling. He completed his exam feeling confident and in control, earning not only a brand new driver's license, but a big, sweaty handshake from Mr. Wade (who, strangely enough, now seemed to be fully dressed).

Just because you have a piece of paper saying you are allowed to drive, this doesn't mean that, overnight, you are ready to take on rush hour traffic, a highway in a rainstorm, or an hours-long trip. The problem with many freshly-licensed drivers is that they are itching to prove they can do anything. The itch is often so great that it leads to accidents. According to statistics, one out of every three teens will have an accident in their first two years of driving.

These facts are so obvious that many states are toughening up laws to make roads more secure for drivers of

Passing one's driving test is a very exciting experience.

Statistics show that one out of every three teens will have an accident in his or her first two years of driving.

all ages. In New Hampshire, for example, a law passed in 1997 requires sixteen-year-old drivers to wait ninety days after obtaining their license before they can drive alone. During this period, teens must have someone twenty-five years of age or older in the front seat with them. In order to cut down on distractions, drivers are also limited as to the number of other passengers that can ride with them. The purpose of this law is to give young, inexperienced drivers more time to develop the on-the-road experience that will help them avoid crashes.

The truth is that these days there is more traffic, cars are more powerful, and there are more driving distractions—from cell phones and CD players (inside the car) to electric billboards and an increase in bike riders (outside the car)—than ever before. All this makes driving a more complicated activity than ever before. Especially if you are sixteen or seventeen. Although rain, snow, or other kids in the car can contribute to accidents, the biggest cause of all is simply being in a dangerous situation and not having the reflexes or experience to get out of it.

Chapter Two

So You Want a Car?

In few other countries is having a car so important—and so common—as in the United States. Teens in large European cities with old winding streets are much more likely to ride subways or streetcars than think about the hassle of driving or parking a car. Teens in countries where money is scarce and where a car is a mega expenditure might be more likely to ride buses, bikes, or even donkeys, llamas, or camels than to dream about zooming around in a car.

Here, however, cars are a major part of American lifestyle and culture. Ever since Henry Ford began rolling cars off of factory assembly lines, automobiles have been not only mass-produced but—over time—produced for the masses. There are few places in the world where you can buy a car as cheaply as you can in the United States. There are also few places where people have so many cars. It is not unusual for a middle class suburban family to have three cars—one for Dad, one for Mom, one for the kids. This is because in big, sprawling, spread out America, with its miles and miles of highways and byways, there is no better way—and often no other way—to get around. And as a people, Americans are the most mobile society on the planet. Whether zooming across town or across the country, we are constantly on the move.

In America, a car is a symbol of freedom. Climb inside, buckle up, and you can drive from the Pacific to the Atlantic. If you are really in search of new horizons, you can even drive from the tip of Alaska to the tip of Argentina. Is it a coincidence that Americans invented the name and concept of the "freeway"?

Bearing all of the above in mind, it is no wonder that unless you live in downtown Manhattan (where parking in a garage can cost around $10 an hour!), the minute you get your license, you are probably going to want some wheels. Of course, if you are lucky (and strapped for cash—as most normal teens are), your parents will let you drive the family car. However, if you have a part-time job, generous parents, or both, you might think of the possibility of acquiring your very own car.

Used cars are cheaper than new ones, but they usually don't come with state-of-the-art features—or guarantees.

Choosing and Buying a Car

The car of your dreams is probably shiny, state-of-the-art, top-of-the-line, and brand new. Unfortunately, such characteristics also make the car of your dreams downright expensive. Buying a new car ensures that the vehicle is in top condition and comes complete with the latest features (not to mention guarantees). However, many teens—especially if they are footing the entire or part of the cost themselves—might consider buying a used car, either from a used car dealer or from an individual.

Insurance

Driving without automobile insurance is about the craziest thing anybody can do. No matter how good a driver you are, there is no telling what can happen out there on the road. Because it is better to be safe than sorry, it is also very important to be insured. Having automobile insurance means that if you have an accident, your insurance company will—depending on your coverage—pay part or all of the costs of any damage. Damage can extend to any problems that affect you and your car, other drivers and their cars, and any passengers riding in any of the involved cars.

Because teen drivers have the worst accident rates of any age group, companies tend to charge really high insurance rates for teens. If you're a guy, the rates could be even more expensive. Statistics have shown that—because of their risk-taking nature and a higher tendency to drive while drunk or on drugs—young male drivers get into far more accidents than females.

Debate: Should Teens Own Cars?

Having a car is a sign that you are becoming an adult. Like many other adult activities, however, owning a car entails certain responsibilities. Who should be responsible for paying for a car's insurance, gas, and tune-ups—you or your parents (or both)? Obviously, there are no set rules. Often, it comes down to a negotiation between kids and parents to decide what is (financially) possible and fair. The following are some views on kids owning cars:

My mom said she didn't care if my friends' parents bought them cars. She said I could get a part-time job and make monthly payments on the car I wanted. The only job I could get was at a fast-food dump. I got paid minimum wage and was so exhausted that I barely had time to do my homework. After a month, I barely had enough money for the down payment. So I gave up. My mom just said that it's tough being an adult and you can't have everything you want.—Raina, seventeen

I made a deal with my parents. If they bought me a car, I'd be totally responsible for all the costs, such as insurance fees, the cost of gas, tune-ups, and repairs. When I wrecked my car, I had to pay for the new windshield and passenger side window. Even though it means I have to cut down on other spending, I'm glad to pay because that way I feel my car is really mine and not just some gift from my folks.—Sal, sixteen

I think it's good for teens to contribute to the costs of their cars. It teaches you responsibility on how to manage your money. And if you're paying for your own car, you'll end up taking much better care of it because it is yours. Why should parents pay for a car they don't drive?—Ben, fifteen

I think it's important that a teen pays for some stuff. After all, if we want to be grown-up, we can't expect Mommy and Daddy to pay for everything forever. At the same time, since we're not totally adults yet, it's only fair that our parents help out some. That's part of the price of raising kids.—Lise, sixteen

Maintenance

If you are lucky enough to have your own car, you have to learn how to take care of it. Keeping it in good shape will ensure that your car lasts for a long time with few serious—and seriously expensive—problems. Most important, treating your wheels well will ensure that they don't suddenly fall apart or self-destruct.

Keep your car clean, inside and out. Nothing is more disgusting than stale fries and smelly sneakers in the back seat. On the outside, keep it clean and rust-free. Wash and wax the body from time to time.

Use good quality tires and make sure they are inflated to the right pressure. If you live in a climate that gets a lot of snow, make sure you outfit your vehicle with a set of snow tires for the winter months. Don't let your tires get bald. Lack of traction can prevent you from stopping or could lead to an explosive blowout.

Always check oil, gas, and water levels. At the risk of sounding nuts: Treat your car as if it were a cherished member of your family. Take the old thing in to the garage for a yearly check-up or in the event that it starts coughing smoke, making funny noises, vibrating in weird ways, or simply acting strange. Among other things, a slipping transmission, worn-out brakes, or a hesitant engine could spell real trouble and lead to an eventual accident.

Keep your car clean inside and out with regular washing and waxing.

Chapter Three | Better Safe Than Sorry

If you've ever driven to an airport to catch a plane, you might have spent ample time in the car gnawing on your nails and trying to dismiss the images of the previous week's Tragedy of the Week made-for-TV movie about terrorists bombing a major American airline. The fact is that, based on statistics, you are far more likely to die in a car crash on the way to the airport than you are to die in a plane crash.

All this is to say that accidents will happen—and they do. In order to avoid them, it is not only smart but essential to play it safe. This means that although driving is a kick, a thrill, and so on, it doesn't pay to take dumb risks, drive in uncertain conditions, or put yourself, your passengers, and your car in sticky situations over which you have no control.

Exceeding the legal speed limit set by each state can result in a ticket or even an arrest.

Speeding

Speeding is one of the major causes of accidents, especially when it comes to thrill-seeking speed junkies such as those in your age group. Speeding means exceeding the legal speed limit. This is always posted—although it might change from state to state and be different on city streets than on freeways or country roads. (Although you might complain about being forced to crawl along like a slug, in truth, overall speed limits have increased over the last few years.) Speeding also refers to driving too fast under dangerous conditions, such as icy roads, poorly lit streets, major curves, and steep hills.

A recent survey carried out by the National Highway Traffic Safety Administration (NHTSA) showed that most Americans are die-hard speeders. Close to 66 percent of all drivers admit to occasionally driving over the maximum safe speed on roads they regularly travel. Meanwhile, 23 percent admit to going 10 miles per hour over the speed limit on interstates, and 6 percent admit to racing other drivers. As for why they speed, 44 percent do so because they are running late for an appointment; 12 percent feel they have to keep up with the rest of traffic (most of which, coincidentally, is also speeding); while 11 percent claim they have bonafide emergencies.

Falling Asleep at the Wheel

Fatigue—or sleepiness—might not seem like such a dangerous thing. However, it can dull your reaction time and make you less aware of what is going on around you. Sleepiness can sneak up on you at any time, but driving late at night is particularly risky. After a long day at school or driving home from a party, many a teen has fallen asleep at the wheel and woken up (if lucky!) with his or her car wrapped around a tree. Signs that you might doze off along the road include yawning a lot, difficulty keeping your eyes open, trouble paying attention to the road, inability to remember the last few seconds, and your car wandering into another lane or onto the shoulder of the road.

The minute you feel yourself nodding off, pull off

Driving while sleepy is often deadly. If you are very tired, *do not drive.*

the road as soon as possible. If you are alone, park your car in a safe place. Then call home or a friend to see if someone more awake can come and pick you up. If you aren't alone, change drivers. If none of these suggestions are options, stop as soon as you can and stock up on caffeine drinks such as coffee, tea, or soda. Roll down the windows and let the cool wind blast you. Turn on the radio and let some loud hip-hop music blast you.

A Scary Stat

Even though there are fewer drivers on U.S. roads at night, according to the government's national accident database, the risk of death in a traffic accident

31

more than doubles when darkness falls. In 1996, more than 18,000 drivers or passengers, 3,500 pedestrians, and 368 cyclists were killed as the result of nighttime car crashes.

A Refreshing Idea

Down Under—in Australia, to be precise—people whose eyes are glazing over can pull into "Driver Reviver" stops. Long-distance drivers can stretch their legs and load up on free coffee or tea, accompanied by a chocolate bar.

Tricky Weather

Whether you're dealing with rain or snow, sleet or hail, fog or mist, wacky weather can change road conditions and make driving risky. Visibility can be reduced, and your car might slip, skid, or slide. If you absolutely must drive in bad weather, then do so at a reduced speed and with extreme caution. Double the space between you and the car in front of you since your brakes take longer to kick in on slippery roads. The following are some important things to remember:

- If weird weather is in the air, stay tuned to the radio so you can avoid any trouble spots.

- Whenever you need to use windshield wipers— during rain, snow, monsoon, or typhoon— make sure your headlights are on. Not only will this increase your visibility, but it will allow other drivers to see you.

+ Don't go out driving in a winter wonderland without bringing along an ice scraper, a brush, and wiper fluid/de-icer.

+ Don't even try passing another car if the weather is bad.

+ If you get stuck in ice or snow, try sliding your floor mats under the tires in order to give them traction.

Fatal Distractions

A surprising number of car accidents occur because drivers simply "weren't paying attention." The problem is that most Americans—particularly young ones—just aren't content to sit in their cars and drive them from A to B. They have to change the radio station every five minutes, take bites from the hamburger sitting on the dashboard (American drivers eat an annual average of thirteen meals in their cars), gab on cell phones (you have four times as many chances of smashing up your car while chatting on the phone), reset the CD in the player, yak it up with the three friends sitting beside and behind them, smooch their boyfriends, fight with their girlfriends . . . the list goes on and on.

Distracted drivers are far more likely to get into accidents, so when you drive, keep your eyes and mind on the road.

Needless to say, doing more than one thing—namely driving—in the car is not such a good idea. If you absolutely have to yak on the phone, change the CD, comb your hair, give your boyfriend a hickey, slap your little brother, eat four french fries, break down and bawl, or check your e-mail on your dashboard-installed PC—(according to the experts, this will be the big car gadget of the early twenty-first century)—pull onto the shoulder or into a parking lot first.

Chapter Four

Drinking and Driving

*A*s a reward for getting his license, Mel's dad bought him a brand-new convertible. "Wow, Dad! It's fly!" yelled Mel in delight. "No, son. It's a car," responded Mel's father, giving his son a funny look.

Vocabulary aside, Mel couldn't wait to show off his new car to the guys at school. Mel was kind of shy, but he was sure that his swank new car would be a good ice-breaker. Hopefully it would give his reputation a bit of a boost as well. Last week at his locker, he had overheard the guys talking about some "dweeb"—it turned out that the dweeb was named Mel. Although he couldn't be sure—there might just be another Mel enrolled at his high school—Mel had a sneaking suspicion that he was the dweeb in question.

Having a brand-new car may make you the envy of your friends, but it's still a big responsibility.

After school, Mel tore out of class, leapt into his parked car, and waited eagerly for the guys to come out of the school building. At the last minute, he remembered to don some cool aviator shades. Just in time, too! He saw the guys striding across the parking lot. "Hey, guys!" called Mel. Although he was sure that they would come over and check out his car, the guys surprised him by muttering "Heys" in his direction and walking away.

Thinking the guys hadn't seen his new car because of the glare of the late afternoon sun, Mel screeched out of the parking lot in hopes of catching up to them. "Hey, guys!" he yelled, pulling alongside the guys. "Can I give you dudes a lift in my boss new car?"

Vincent started to say no, but Jim punched him in the shoulder. "Sure, man," said Jim, opening up the back door. "I could go for a little afterschool spin in this clunker."

"Come on, guys," he motioned to Vincent, Ellsworth, and Pablo. "It'll be cool to have some wheels for a change."

Once they all were inside the car, Mel put his foot on the gas. It felt great to be in his new car with his new buds. "Where to, guys?" he shouted. "I really wanna rock out."

The guys exchanged glances. "Let's just cruise, man," suggested Vincent. "I've got a bottle of Jack on me." He yanked a flask out of his knapsack, took a swig, and passed it around.

When the flask came to Mel, he hesitated. But when he saw Jim beside him, with a scornful look on his face, he tipped his head back and let the liquor burn down his throat. He gagged, and the guys snickered. Angry, Mel took another gulp and stepped on the accelerator. He'd show the guys that he wasn't a dweeb.

Mel sped through residential side streets and then turned onto the main boulevard. All the time the flask got passed around. Thinking they were watching to see how much he swallowed,

Mel took big, manly gulps of the alcohol. Every time he took a swig, the guys roared with laughter. Mel decided they must be having a good time with him.

On the main boulevard, Mel zigzagged from lane to lane, passing cars that were driving too slow. Even though it was getting dark, he decided to keep his shades on in order to look cooler. His head began to feel light and he found himself laughing uproariously with the guys, although he wasn't sure at what.

"Hey, dweeb!" yelled Pablo from the backseat. "I gotta take a leak. Turn left at the next light. There's a park where I can whizz."

Mel must have misunderstood Pablo. Had he really called him a "dweeb"? He turned sharply to the left and the car skidded into a side street.

"Take it easy, bro," said Jim beside him. But Mel just wanted to show them that he wasn't a dweeb. With the gas pedal to the floor, the car shrieked down the street. The guys started screaming at Mel to slow down. Through his shades, Mel saw a dark mass in front of him that he thought must be the park. Funny that the park was dark, thought Mel to himself. A dark park.

Then suddenly, there was a big shape in the road in front of him. It looked like a person. The

Never get into a car with *anyone* who has been drinking or let anyone who has been drinking attempt to drive.

*guys were shouting as Mel turned the wheel fran-
tically. The car went lurching . . . straight into a
massive oak tree.*

*Nobody got a chance to call Mel a dweeb
ever again.*

You have probably heard about the dangers of drinking and driving. Over and over again. The problem isn't
ignorance. The problem is self-control and self-
discipline. It is not giving in to peer pressure. Ever. It is
not an issue of how much you drink. You shouldn't
drink at all if there is any chance of you getting into a
car and driving. Moreover, you shouldn't get into a car
with anyone you even remotely suspect has been drinking—whether a teen or an adult. Beyond this, you
shouldn't even let anyone you remotely suspect has
been drinking get into a car and attempt to drive it—
even if you're not going to be along for the ride.

Alcohol—even a small amount—dulls your senses
and reflexes, impairs your visibility, distracts you, and
makes you hyper, drowsy, or aggressive. The same
goes for any kind of drug, even prescription and over-
the-counter medication (always check labels for side
effects). In short, they make you a serious menace to
yourself, to any passengers dumb enough to be riding
with you, and to any other drivers, cyclists, pedestrians,
dogs, cats, or trees unlucky enough to come into contact with you in your drunken state.

Spotting a Drunk Driver

You can bet your rear bumper that a driver is drunk if you catch him or her doing one or more of the following:

- Weaving in and out of lanes or across the road
- Keeping his or her face close to the windshield
- Driving off the road
- Swerving or turning suddenly
- Stopping for no reason in the middle of traffic
- Following other cars too closely
- Ignoring traffic signals
- Sudden speeding up or slowing down
- Driving without headlights

The NHTSA estimates that alcohol is involved in close to 25 percent of fatal car crashes. In 1994, this translated to 16,589 deaths due to drinking and driving—or one every thirty-two minutes! In protest, groups such as Students Against Drunk Driving (SADD) and Mothers Against Drunk Driving (MADD) have sprung up all across North America. At the same time—as a response to outraged communities—states have beefed up police checkpoints, toughened laws, and cracked down on young drivers with any level of alcohol in their system by suspending their licenses.

Some more startling statistics about alcohol and driving that you should know include:

- Four out of ten Americans will be involved in an alcohol-related crash at some point in their lives.

- Every day, eight young people die in alcohol-related crashes.

- 40 percent of all sixteen-to-twenty-year-olds who died in 1994 were killed in car crashes. Half of those crashes were alcohol-related.

A SADD Story

In 1981, in the space of two weeks, two female students at a small Massachusetts high school were killed as a result of drunken driving. These tragic deaths led the students, aided by their hockey coach Robert Anastas, to form a group dedicated to fighting the number one killer of teenagers in the United States.

Realizing that it was important for parents to get involved, Anastas developed the "Contract for Life." This was a document, signed by both teens and parents, in which each promised to help the other in extreme situations. For instance, let's say you went to a party and got drunk, and then didn't want to risk driving home and having an accident. According to the contract, you could call your parents—at whatever time, wherever you were—and they would come and pick

Set up an agreement with your parents, allowing them to pick you up—no questions asked—if you have had too much to drink.

you up—no questions asked. At the same time, in signing the contract, you also had to recognize that drinking and doing drugs is illegal and that your parents have the right to deal with you at a later date.

The "Contract for Life," and SADD itself (whose name was later changed to Students Against Destructive Decisions) caught on big time. Both public and private financial support allowed it to spread across the nation and help prevent teens from drinking and driving. The happy ending to this SADD story is that between 1988 and 1998, the number of young drivers involved in fatal car crashes who were drunk actually decreased—by a whopping 33 percent.

Designated Drivers

Programs such as SADD and MADD have done a great deal to make students aware of the dangers of drinking and driving. At the same time, teens will be teens: The number of you who reach the age of twenty-one without ever having had a drop of alcohol is small. No matter what age you are, it is dumb to drink and drive.

But if you do end up getting dragged to a party where you know that alcohol will be on hand—make sure that you bring along a designated driver. A designated driver is a pal who vows not to get into the liquor (or drugs) at all, but instead to round up you and all your buds and deposit you safely at home at the end of the evening. Treat your designated driver like a prince (or princess) by treating him or her to delicious nonalcoholic cocktails and munchies. Because fair is fair, promise him or her that the next party that comes around you'll do the driving, and he or she can do the drinking (if he or she desires).

Chapter Five | Raging Down the Road

At the same time that accidents due to drinking and driving have been on the decline, a new crash-causing phenomenon has reared its ugly head on America's highways and byways: road rage. Road rage means getting in your car and taking out all your stress and anger on other drivers. It can be expressed in a number of ways: speeding, tailgating, horn-honking, shouting, finger-flipping, cutting off another car, bashing into another car, forcing another car off the road. If in the last ten years, accidents due to drunk driving have gone down by close to 40 percent, those due to road rage have skyrocketed—increasing at a rate of 7 percent a year.

People and Their Cars

Earlier on in this book we looked at how important cars have become in Americans' lives. As agents of freedom and mobility, cars have had a very positive impact on American lifestyle. But there has been a downside to car culture as well. A car is not only an object of convenience, beauty, and status. It is also a psychological object—that is, an unconscious extension of a person's sense of self. As such, when you climb into a car, it is like being in a protective and powerful shell. The wonderful thing about a car is you can control it and it can serve you well when you are trying to get from A to B. However, when other people in other cars are clogging up the same roads trying to get from A to B as well, this creates conflict.

> *Leni is in a hurry. As she races down the highway, the road is clear. She zooms around a sharp curve, and suddenly, there's a big truck in front of her. It seems to be travelling at twenty-five miles an hour and is blowing black exhaust fumes into her face. Leni reduces speed and immediately feels frustrated. She suddenly has no control. All because of the truck-driver jerk, she will be late for meeting her boyfriend. There is nothing she can do to get past this truck. It is dangerous to pass. She honks her horn a few times. Nothing happens. Leni is*

*fuming now and getting angrier and more frus-
trated by the minute. After fifteen minutes, her
anger gets the best of her. Not caring about any
danger, she decides to pass the truck. As she speeds
by—just missing an oncoming car—she gives the
truck-driver jerk the finger to let him know how he
ruined her day.*

Leni's situation is increasingly common. The fact is
that in the last ten years, while the number of cars on
the road has increased by 35 percent, the number of
new roads constructed has increased by only 1 percent. This means more traffic, more traffic jams, and
more people getting angry. At the same time, life has
become more stressful. Think of your life. You might
have parents and teachers breathing down your back,
homework and essays galore, doubts about colleges or
careers, peer pressure, and all sorts of other daily
pressure. Some people take out their stress when they
are safely behind the wheel of their car. They do so by
driving aggressively.

Road Rage

You aren't born with road rage, and you can't inherit
it either. Road rage is a series of reactions and attitudes that anybody can learn. It depends on the culture to which you are exposed. And unfortunately, our

Road rage and aggressive driving are very dangerous and are not effective ways to handle the stress of driving in traffic.

culture—full of crash-'em-up-smash-'em-up video games, television series in which cop cars screech around city corners after crooks, and action films in which audiences cheer when the hero, in a heated drag race, succeeds in forcing the bad guy's car over a cliff and into flames—glorifies road rage.

Even normally sweet, kind, shy people can turn into raving Rambos if another driver cuts in front of them unexpectedly. Think about when you were younger, driving around with your parents. Can you recall your normally calm and in-control mother shaking her fist and swearing at the guy who "stole" her parking space at the supermarket? Chances are, outside of her car she would never react so violently. But the problem is that long before they end up in the driver's seat themselves, most kids have learned such behavior from their parents.

Many experts feel that this aggressive attitude to driving is reinforced by driver's ed courses. This is because most courses use an approach called defensive driving, in which students are to be on their guard against "bad drivers" and assume that every other driver on the road is a potential enemy. Consider the following facts:

- Aggressive behavior—ranging from honking and yelling to exchange of gunfire—is a factor in more than 28,000 deaths and 1 million injuries a year.

Much of our entertainment culture seems to glorify aggression and violence, especially behind the wheel.

- It is estimated that 53 percent of American drivers have "road rage disorder."

- In the last year, 48 percent of drivers received rude gestures, 16 percent were victims of verbal abuse, and 1 percent were physically assaulted.

Keeping Cool on the Way to School

To make a mistake is both common and human. So it is crazy to expect that a complicated activity such as driving could be error-free. Because more people have access to cars than ever before, this means that streets are filled with all kinds of drivers with different attitudes and ways of dealing with emotions. Obviously, the vast majority are not going to be perfect drivers. Some might be old and therefore cautious. Others might come from another state or country. They might be unfamiliar with busy city roads and find it difficult to react to so many things so quickly.

Instead of getting mad at these "dumb" drivers for screwing up or getting in your way, try to cut other drivers some slack if they screw up. It will cause both you and everybody else on the road less stress if you check your impulse to rant and rave every time you encounter a slow driver in the passing lane.

Aside from changing your thinking—maybe the person who braked too suddenly in front of you is not a complete moron for almost causing your coffee to spill all over the dashboard, but a father who was perhaps distracted by his two young kids in the backseat—there are other things you can do to keep cool in the car.

- Allow yourself plenty of time to get to your destination. If you aren't stressed that you will be late for school, you will be a lot more relaxed and enjoy your trip more.

- Don't react to aggressive drivers. If someone is yelling at you, close your window and avoid eye contact.

- Try to use your horn as little as possible (honking can rile some drivers).

- Create a laid-back atmosphere in your car. Play relaxing music. Hang a sweet-smelling auto sachet from your rearview mirror. (Britain's Automobile Association is exploring the use of aromatherapy to reduce road rage through a device that circulates fragrant oils throughout the car to soothe drivers.)

In general, if you're generous and patient with other drivers, they will return the favor. (If you're a road hog, others will be provoked and try to mess with you.) Always remember that you might own your car—but you don't own the road.

Conclusion

The fact that car crashes are the leading cause of death for young Americans between the ages of fifteen and twenty is a chilling thought. Like everything in life, driving requires practice and experience. In fact, experts calculate that it takes the average new driver between five and seven years to get to the point where he or she has sufficient experience to be a king or queen of the road. In those five to seven years, young drivers learn to judge tricky situations and acquire the skills necessary to deal with them.

If such a thought overwhelms you, don't let it. If driving were too easy, it wouldn't be a challenge. It also

It's fun to take a spontaneous road trip with a friend.

wouldn't be fun. And despite the day-to-day hassles of traffic jams and lack of parking and road hogs, there are many times in which being in a car can be a really enjoyable experience. Think of greeting a sunrise on a country backroad; taking a roadtrip across the country with a couple of good friends, a map, and some CDs to sing along to. For better or for worse, cars are a big part of our lives. Learn to use them well and our lives will be that much better.

Glossary

aromatherapy Relaxation technique using fragrant oils from herbs and flowers.

designated driver Person chosen to drive based on the fact that he or she will not drink alcohol.

driver's education Theoretical and practical driving courses taken before obtaining a license.

fatigue Tiredness.

freeway Highway with no toll charges.

parallel parking Manner of parking, in single line, between two cars on a street alongside a curb.

road rage Phenomenon of drivers taking out aggression and stress on other drivers.

skid To slip sideways because of a lack of traction.

Where to Go for Help

In the United States

American Automobile Association Foundation for
    Traffic Safety
1440 New York Avenue NW, Suite 201
Washington, DC 20005
(202) 638-5944
(800) 305-SAFE
Web site: http://www.aaafts.org

American Driver and Traffic Safety
    Education Association
Indiana University of Pennsylvania, R & P Building
Indiana, PA 15705
(800) 896-7703
Web site: http://adtsea.iup.edu/adtsea

MADD (Mothers Against Drunk Driving)
P.O. Box 541688
Dallas, TX 75354-1688
(800) GET-MADD
Web site: http://www.madd.org

National Commission Against Drunk Driving
1900 L Street NW, Suite 705
Washington, DC 20006
(202) 452-6004
Web site: http://www.ncadd.com

National Highway Traffic Safety Administration (NHTSA)
400 7th Street SW
Washington, DC 20590
Web site: http://www.nhtsa.dot.gov

National Safety Council
1121 Spring Lake Drive
Itasca, IL 60143-3201
(630) 285-1121
Web site: http://www.nsc.org

In Canada

Canada Safety Council
1020 Thomas Spratt Place
Ottawa, ON K1G 5L5

(613) 739-1535
Web site: http://www.safety-council.org

Canadian Automobile Association
1145 Hunt Club Road, Suite 200
Ottawa, ON K1V 0Y3
(613) 247-0117
Web site: http://www.caa.ca

MADD Canada
6507C Mississauga Road
Mississauga, ON L5N 1A6
(800) 665-6233
Web site: http://www.madd.ca

Web Sites

Drivers.com
http://www.drivers.com

SADD Online
http://www.saddonline.com/

Teen New Drivers' Homepage
http://www.teendriving.com

YARR (Youth Against Road Rage)
http://www.aloha.net/~dyc/yarr

For Further Reading

Bauer, Joan. *Rules of the Road.* New York: Penguin
   Putnam Books, 1999.
Berardelli, Phil. *Safe Young Drivers: A Guide for
   Parents and Teens.* Baltimore, MD: Nautilus
   Communications, 1996.
Biardo, John C. *The Safe Driving Handbook: A Guide
   to Driving Defensively.* Chicago, IL: Elmwood Park
   Publishing, 1996.
Cooney, Caroline B. *Driver's Ed.* New York: Bantam
   Doubleday Dell Publishing Group, 1995.
Coy, John. *Night Driving.* New York: Henry Holt and
   Company, 1996.
Grosshandler, Janet. *Coping with Drinking and
   Driving.* New York: Rosen Publishing Group, 1997.
Jennings, Jean Lindamood (ed.) *Road Trips, Head*

Trips, and Other Car-Crazed Writings. New York: Atlantic Monthly Press, 1998.

Lynch, Chris. *Political Timber.* New York: Harper-Collins Publishers, 1997.

Magliozzi, Tom. *Car Talk: With Click and Clack, the Tappet Brothers.* New York: Bantam Doubleday Dell, 1996.

Pease, Robert A. *How to Drive into Accidents—and How Not To.* New York: Pease Publishing, 1999.

Wong, Janet S. *Behind the Wheel: Driving Poems.* New York: Margaret McElderry Books, 1999.

Index

About the Author

Adam Winters is a freelance journalist who lives on a farm in Texas.

Photo Credits

Cover by Maura Boruchow; p. 2 and p. 18 © Superstock; pp. 8, 17, 22, 27, 29, 31, 34, 37, 40, 44, and 49 by Maura Boruchow; p. 12 © Dan Lamont/Corbis; p. 51 © International Stock; p. 54 © Edward L. Miller/Stock, Boston/PictureQuest.

Layout

Danielle Goldblatt